STORIES TOLD IN THE KITCHEN

North Country Press • Unity, Maine

Library of Congress Cataloging in Publication Data:

Morse, Kendall, 1934–
Stories told in the kitchen.

I. Title.
PS3563.O88124S78 813'.54 81-8775
ISBN 0-945980-19-1 AACR2
(Formerly ISBN 0-89621-064-2 (pbk.))

Fifth printing.

Dedication

To Gordon Bok, who first
suggested it ten years ago . . .

Foreword

Kendall Morse and Tim Sample have combined their considerable talents to produce for the first time ever a really fine illustrated compendium of Maine humor. The core of the collection comes from Kendall's memories of his youth in Machias and of his famous storyteller uncle, Curt Morse. Also, a great many of Kendall's stories have come from his days as the captain of a sizeable vessel plying the Maine coast. More recently, he has gathered still more stories in his travels across the nation as a folk singer and storyteller.

Kendall has done a great deal to revive the interest in Maine storytelling in Gordon Wark's public broadcasting production *In the Kitchen.* The programs, seven in all, were an enormous success from coast to coast. Californians, Georgians, Texans and Oregonians were astounded and delighted week after week when they peered at their television sets to see two rustic types sitting in an old-fashioned kitchen speaking to each other with the oddest accent, recounting the most outrageous stories. Each week Kendall would engage a different Maine storyteller in conversation (Bruce McGorill, Donald Taverner, Henry Hatch, Joseph Perham, myself, Sandy Ives and Bill Gagnon) over coffee and doughnuts as if they were old cronies discussing the day's events. It was the ideal vehicle for airing the best of each storyteller's repertoire, and it is from these programs that Kendall has drawn some of the better stories in this book.

With the television series *In the Kitchen* the Maine storytelling tradition had gone national once more. Americans are all too familiar with Appalachian hillbillies and Texas cowboys and their sense of humor, but our American citizenry long ago lost touch with the State of Maine. Not since D. W. Griffith's film *Way Down East* and Richard Golden's melodrama *Old Jed Prouty* have Americans received such a powerful dose of Maine culture.

This book will reinforce the effects of the television programs. Its techniques are similar. The tales in the book are cleverly "folded in" to everyday conversations and events in a small Maine community. The stories are incorporated into a large story which comprises the book itself. The awkwardness of a joke telling session with its succession of unconnected anecdotes is neatly avoided. The book will have a wide national circulation, make no mistake, not only because of the hilarity of the stories, but because of the skill with which they are told.

Tim Sample's illustrations sound just the right note to accompany the stories. They enhance the zany, mapcap quality. In this book, Morse and Sample have let the cat out of the bag. They have shown that Maine's cool sanity rests firmly on its ability to go insane at will.

Marshall Dodge

In Appreciation

For great fun and some fabulous yarns, the author thanks those who participated with him on the *In the Kitchen* series: Marshall Dodge, Bruce McGorrill, Don Taverner, Joe Perham, Henry Hatch, Bill Gagnon, and Edward "Sandy" Ives. Thanks also to the other good friends and talented storytellers, too numerous to mention, who have shared and kept humor alive in the State of Maine.

I live about two miles up the Ebb Tide Road in a house that was built by my grandfather. It's well over a hundred years old, and will probably be around for another hundred. Houses don't have many natural enemies in Marshall's Landing.

Me and the missus and our three girls live here year-round, if you can call it living. The summer is real nice, what with the sea breeze and all, but the winter gets quite savagrus by times.

There are four rooms downstairs and three up, but in the winter, we close off one of the downstairs rooms to save on heat, so we spend a lot of time in the kitchen. The parlor is reserved for important company, such as the preacher and the ladies sewing circle.

The old kitchen is pretty much as it was when Mother

was alive, though we did swap the old hand pump on the sink for an electric pump in the cellar, and the old ice box went to the dump years ago, having been replaced by a refrigerator. For entertainment, we rely pretty much on ourselves, and one of the things we enjoy most is having someone drop in for an evening of checkers or just yarning.

It was colder than a dead man's tongue, and I was sitting around trying to keep my pipe going, when I heard someone stamping the snow off his feet on the front steps. The piazza is on the front of the house, facing south. In the summer it's a nice place to sit and watch the boats coming and going out in the harbor, and, in the winter, having the front door face south helps keep the heat in when someone goes in or out. Around here the north wind is called the Montreal Express, and if the door was on the north side it would blow the dishes off the table and quick freeze whatever was on them at the same time.

I wasn't expecting anyone, so, when I opened the door I was both surprized and pleased to see Grover Furlong standing there with an icicle hanging off the tip of his long nose.

"Godfry mighty, Grover!" I said. "What are you doing out on a rafter snapper night like this?"

"Didn't realize how cold it was. Broke my glasses and can't see the thermometer. That mercury is getting shorter and harder to read every day now," he answered. "Besides," he added, "The old woman was getting on my nerves jawing about one thing and another all the time."

"That woman's got more mouth than a government mule."

" 'Course, I don't help much. When she gets started,

sometimes I keep her going. This morning I called her 'Angel' and when she asked why, I told her it was because she was always up in the air harping about something, and she hasn't run down yet."

"Come in, Grover," I said. "I was just about to put the tea pot on."

Now, making a pot of tea is not a casual undertaking at my house. None of those tea bags for me. Those are for lazy folks and those who never learned to do it right. I take a handful of black tea, drop it into a pot of boiling water, and then move it to the back of the stove and let it steep for as long as it takes. After it sets there for two or three hours, you have to poke a hole in it to put the milk in, but a slug of that tea is more than a match for the chill-blains.

Grover took off his Mackinaw and hung it on the back

of his chair, rolled up the ear tabs on his cap, sat down and took a swig of that tea.

"I never drink tea but what I think of that feller over to Thorndike. Name was Fletcher Elkhorn, and I don't think he ever said more than a dozen words in the forty-odd years I knew him.

"He used to come into the snack bar every day around noon and order a cup of tea. Without fail, he would complain that it was not hot enough. Finally, one of the girls decided to see if she could make a cup of tea which would satisfy the old grouch, so around 11:30 one morning, she put a cup in the oven and baked it at 300 degrees for half an hour. When the old man came in at noon, she poured boiling tea into that cup and served it to him. He took one sip of that brew, which must have burned his shoe taps, but he would not admit that he had been taken, he just looked at her and said, 'The Fool Killer will be coming to get you tomorrow.' "

While Grover was unlacing his gum rubber boots, I went to the window to check the thermometer.

"I must be getting old," I said. "It's only 8 below zero but it feels more like 40 below."

"It's the wind," Grover said. "Good thing we don't get wind in the winter like some of them summer hurricanes. Hurricane Carol really raised the Old Harry around here. I had a hen at the time, she was laying into the wind and it blew so hard she laid the same egg five times."

"I remember that one," I said. "It blew so hard that it unravelled a crow bar, and blew two rooster feathers right through my grindstone.

"Another cup of tea, Grover?" I asked.

"Might as well," he said, "it looks like a long evening when you get started on them weather yarns."

Grover is Chief Engineer on the tug boat *Half Moon* out of Belfast, and having spent most of his adult life on the sea, I knew he enjoyed both the telling and the hearing of weather tales, so, ignoring his remark, I began to lie in earnest.

"My grandfather, Captain Orrin Hathway," I began, "was in the three masted schooner *Emily Beal* at the time. This was, oh, 60 or 70 years ago. Her home port was Portland, Maine, and she was three days overdue with a cargo of Cod fish from the Grand Banks. Two days from port the wind died out and she just sat there, loaded to the deadeyes, wallowing in the trough, slatting her gear to pieces with her cargo in danger of rotting in the hold. Old Captain Orrin put up with this for one whole day before his patience ran out, but finally, at the end of his rope, he began to walk the quarter-deck and swear. He knew more cuss words than any Nova Scotia sailor I ever met, and, as you know, those Nova Scotia boys are champion blasphemers.

"After about twenty minutes of uttering obscenity and profanity, he took out a silver dollar, held it up, and addressing all the Gods who might be on duty, he said,

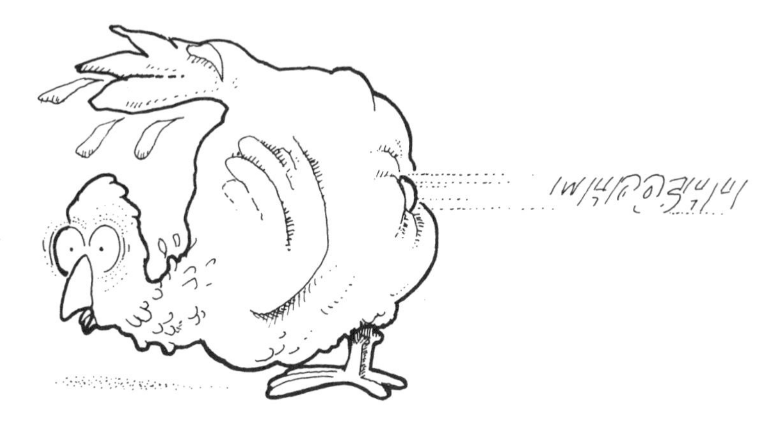

'Damn it all, sell me some wind, will you?' He then threw that dollar into the air, and it had no more than hit the water when the wind began to blow a living judgement. It took the masts, sails and rigging over the side and turned the life boats into useless pieces of wood.

"The gale drove her ashore just south of Cape Elizabeth, where she pounded herself to kindling in the surf and ledges. The whole crew made it to shore somehow, and after they got their bearings, one of them said, 'Well Skipper, looks like you got your wind!'

"Looking at the remains of his ship and cargo the old man just said, 'Yes — but if I'd known that wind was so cheap, I wouldn't have ordered so much.' "

A long silence followed while Grover stirred his third cup of tea. Finally, he looked me right in the face and eyes and said, "If I owed the Devil a thousand liars, and he wouldn't take you as a down payment, I'd think him a hard one to deal with."

"Grover," I said, "if I ever start telling the truth, it's going to take a lot of the fun out of it. But speaking of lies, my Uncle Curtis always insisted that he met up with a Timber Rattler up in Washington County many years ago. The way he used to tell it was: 'I was just getting ready to shove off, and I had everything I needed loaded into the canoe, when I noticed that I had forgotten the bait. Well, here I am miles from any place where I could get bait and wondering what to do about it. While I'm pondering the situation, I happened to look down, and there in the underbrush was a big rattler with a frog in its mouth. Of course, frogs are excellent bait, but I really didn't want to take it away from the snake, so I took my jug of hard cider and poured some of it on that snake's head. It dropped the frog, and crawled off into the

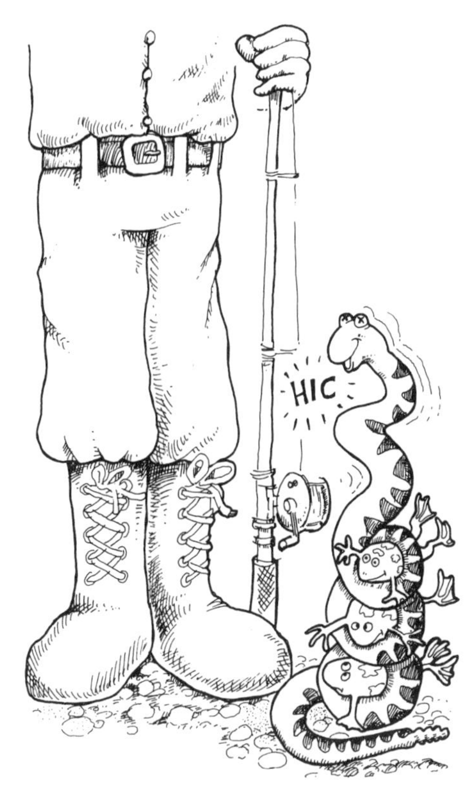

bushes. Well, I puttered around some, finished loading the gear and all, and I was just about to step into the canoe when I felt something hit my boot. I looked down, and there was that snake back with three more frogs!' "

"Uncle!" I said. "Everyone knows that Timber Rattlers have been extinct in Maine for two hundred years. That must have been the last of its kind."

"All Uncle Curtis said was, 'No wonder it had a drinking problem.' "

"Speaking of drinking problems, Grover, I've got about

five gallons of hard cider left over from last fall. Would you like a little snort of it?"

"I certainly would," he answered, "but I hope it's better than that last batch you made. One swallow of that would make you walk a barbed wire fence barefoot with a Wildcat under each arm."

By the time I returned from the cellar with the cider, Grover was waiting with a big tumbler and another story.

"There is something about hard cider and fishing trips. They just naturally go together. While you were down cellar I got to thinking about that fishing trip up to Bear Brook. It's been all of thirty years now, but Gorry, that was a big trout I caught. When I pulled him out of the water, it took twenty minutes for the hole it left to fill up again.

"I knew it was going to take a big set of scales to weight it so I hauled it into the town of Fayette, but there wasn't a set of scales anywhere in town that could handle it, so Dick Pelletier took a picture of it, and the negative weighed fourteen pounds."

"Ayuh." I said, "I suppose now you're going tò tell me its name was Moby Dick."

"Funny you should mention Bear Brook," I said. "Years ago a bunch of us had a camp up in that country that we used for hunting and fishing trips. I was just recalling the time we were in there with that bunch of fellows from New York on a deer hunting trip. Do you remember that young lawyer that we called Pettifogger?"

"No, I don't think I do," said Grover, searching his memory.

"Well, maybe you wasn't there on that particular trip.

I used to get a big kick out of sending greenhorns like him out to the spring for water after dark. Always figured that was a good way to introduce them to the Maine Woods. He was right out of the middle of New York City, and had never been in Maine before, and, of course, he was scared half to death of getting eaten up by some Side Hill Gouger, a Tree Squeak or some other horrible creature which we had told him about.

"Anyway, it was some dark about ten that night when I told him it was the custom for the newest member of the party to get a pail of water from the spring for morning coffee. The last thing in the world he wanted to do was to venture outside that camp at night, but he knew if he refused he would never live it down, so he grabbed the bucket and headed out the door.

"Not more than a minute later, he came busting in all

feather white and out of breath. His eyes looked like two boiled onions, and I never saw anyone so terrified in my life.

" 'What in Tofit ails you?' I asked, knowing all along that he had probably heard a noise he couldn't identify.

"When he had recovered enough wind to speak he stammered 'There's a huge black bear in the water!'

"After we all had a good laugh at his expense, I said to him, 'That bear is more afraid of you than you are of him.'

'Well, if that's true, that water ain't fit to drink anyway,' he said."

About that time my old grandfather clock struck nine and Grover remarked, "That old clock is nice to have around, but it keeps reminding folks that time keeps moving even when we don't want it to. My father used to tell about a lobster fisherman down to Cundy's Harbor who had an old grandfather clock for years. Kept perfect time, but one night it went haywire and struck fourteen times. The old man jumped up out of his easy chair and said to his wife 'By thunder let's get to bed, I've never known it to be so late!' "

With that, Grover pulled on his boots and Mackinaw and headed for the door. "You don't have to rush on my account," I said, "it's only nine o'clock."

"Got to get a good night's sleep. Tomorrow we are going to work on the engine in the tugboat. Ever since we pulled that yacht off Hog Island bar last summer she has been vibrating more than she should. I think we must have touched bottom and maybe chipped the wheel. Ever since then the stuffing box keeps leaking, so something must be out of true down there. Never could figure what they were doing in there, ain't enough water there to drown a cat at high tide. The Captain, if you can call him that, said that some clam digger told him there was plenty of water in there. I told him sure there is, but it's just spread kinda thin in spots. He had no sense of humor at all, so when I handed him a bill for towing, I also gave him a copy of Lindsey's Law for future reference."

Lindsey's Law simply states: *When your draft exceeds the depth of the water, you are most assuredly aground.*

"Glad you dropped in, Grover," I said as he was leaving, "bring the wife next time. Watch yourself going down them steps, damned gutter leaked during that mild spell and it's glare ice clear to the road."

Come to think of it, Grover hasn't been back since. Maybe his wife got fed up and brained him. Can't say I blame her, he does plague her something awful.

M
LINDSEY'S LAW
WHEN YOUR DRAFT EXCEEDS THE
DEPTH OF THE WATER.....
...YOU ARE MOST ASSUREDLY
AGROUND!

This morning dawned clear and cold again, and just as I was getting ready to knit some pot heads for sale to the local lobster fishermen, I realized that I was out of tobacco. Going all day without tobacco is like facing the grim spectre of privation to a Half and Half addict like me, so, in spite of the sub-zero weather, I fired up the car and headed down to Ira Crabtree's store. I always said that automobiles were no more designed for this climate than humans were, but with that new Die Hard battery she fired up and got rolling much quicker than I did. Them people that's always lamenting the passing of the good old days never had to crank a Model T, and then bundle up in a buffalo lap robe to keep from freezing to death while they rode two miles to the store.

About half a mile from the store the engine just up and cagged on me. It was so cold that the automatic choke couldn't open, and she just flooded herself solid full of raw gas. While I was wondering how I was going to hold that choke open and turn the engine over at the same time, Junior Farnsworth came along, and, seeing the hood up, he mistrusted something was wrong, so he stopped and wanted to know if I had a problem. I said, "If being stuck in a dead car at 14 below zero, with arms six feet too short is a problem, then yes, I do have a problem."

After we got her started again, Junior stuffed a screwdriver handle down in the carburetor and said I should leave it there until I got home. Folks say he is as numb as a pounded thumb, but he does know something about cars. He said, "Them automatic chokes are just something else to frig up. If it was mine, I'd put a hand choke on her."

He looked quite puzzled when I said, "Maybe I'll just quit smoking, instead."

The store was full of idlers, as usual, all sitting in a circle around the big Station Agent stove, and the odor of neatsfoot oil and over-heated wool clothes reminded me that some things never change. It was almost the same as when I first went there with my father many years ago. The minute we entered the store that day, old John Prince said to my father, "I'll give you two cents and a rusty fish hook for that boy." It nearly scared me to death. He was so strange-looking with his long white beard streaked with tobacco juice, and only one tooth in his head. I didn't know what to think when Father answered, "Daow, I wouldn't want to cheat you. Why, he ain't worth half that price!"

Old John and a few others are gone, now, but the same old stories are still being told by old timers who were teenagers in those days. While I was buying my tobacco, and wondering if anything new ever happened around there, poor old Lizzie Gardner came in all haired up, and said to Ira, "I want to buy a mouse trap. Last night a mouse got into my drawers and chewed all the fringe off my center piece!"

The reaction over by the stove started as a snicker, but soon they were all roaring and slapping their knees while Lizzie stood there working her jaws in silence wondering what they were drinking. Rufe Collins laughed so hard he fell off the chair and bumped his head on the leg of the stove, which only added to the hilarity. Poor old Lizzie left not even suspecting that she had made their day.

After the uproar died down, Rufe, rubbing his head and wiping the tears from his eyes said, "Anyone hadn't ought to laugh, but poor old Lizzie just asks for it."

Taking a chair by the stove and lighting up my pipe, I noticed Uriah Boardman sitting there with his nose in the latest copy of *Time* magazine. "Say, Uriah," I said, "We missed you at the funeral last week. Didn't you know we was planting Emma Davis? First time in my life I ever saw that woman with her mouth shut."

Uriah looked at me over his reading glasses and said, "I heard she died, but thought it might be another false alarm."

That puzzled me, so I asked, "What do you mean, false alarm?"

"Oh, hell, she died once before, about 30 years ago. Always felt sorry for her husband, that woman made his life some miserable, nagged at him day and night. Finally, she up and died. Or so they thought. They used to live way out on the Back Narrows road about 10 miles from town, so when it appeared that she was dead, Eldridge made a coffin and loaded her into it. Got the two sons to help carry her out to the wagon, when they got to the gate post they got a mite careless and bumped the coffin against the post. Well, Emma sat right up, wanted to know what she was doing in a box and lived for another 30 years, nagging and making them all miserable all the time. I understand that this time, as they were lugging her out, Eldridge said to them, 'Mind the post, boys, mind the post.' "

"Now, Uriah," I said, "that's about the most unusual excuse I ever heard for not going to a funeral."

Thinking back a few years I said, "Do you remember Chester Woodcock? I suppose there is probably some-

thing wrong with anyone who sees humor in death, but I can't help remembering the time his wife died. It was right in the middle of haying season, so he no more than got her under the sod when he up and married young Nellie Hawkins from over to Monroe. He needed someone to care for the livestock and put up his dinner pail, you see. Of course, he never would admit that she was young and pretty: he was all business, that one. They stayed home for the honeymoon and went to bed early, as was his custom.

"Well, some of the folks in town decided to have some fun, so a bunch of us gathered outside the house for a shivaree to make sure Chester and Nellie didn't get much sleep. Funny how other folks see the same situation from different points of view. We were having a grand time wishing them well, in a way, when, all of a sudden, out comes Chester, all haired up, and he looked all around and said 'What the hell is the matter with you people? Don't you have any respect for the dead?' "

"Hey, Kendall!" yelled Stan Pinkham from the far corner of the store, "Do you remember Harry Plummer? Used to tell some of the damdest lies you ever heard, and it got to where no one would believe a word he said. I even heard it said that when he wanted his dog to come in, he had to get his wife to call it. Anyway, when his wife died, she went in the night sometime, and next morning he couldn't help but notice that she was gone, o'course, so he went downstairs where his daughter was making breakfast and he said to her, 'Don't bother making breakfast for your mother!' "

"Yes, I remember him well," I replied, "he and his brother used to raise pigs way out on the Back Cove Road. One spring they began to lose pigs one at a time, and he thought it might be on account of a bear, so he sat up all one night with his rifle sticking out of the bedroom window, pointed right at the pig pen. Just before dark he had hung a lantern on the gate post, and he figured that if it was a bear he stood a pretty good chance of getting it. About 3 in the morning he was dozing off, but he came to just in time to see an old she-bear coming out of the pig pen with a shoat under one arm, walking on her hind feet, and holding up the lantern with the other paw. Harry said he drew a bead on that bear's forehead and was just about to squeeze the trigger when that bear turned around and blew out the light."

Ira added, "Not only was he the biggest liar in this town, he was also the worst poacher, too. As a matter of

fact, he bought two pounds of beef steak here just a few days before he died. I asked him how come he was buying meat, and he told me that he was forced into it because the deer out his way were getting too smart. It was always his way to find an apple orchard where the deer tended, and early in the evening he would climb up a tree with his rifle and a five-cell flashlight. After it got dark, the deer would come out and feed. He'd turn on the light, pick out a pair of eyes, aim between them, and shoot. This went on for years, but according to Harry, they finally got smart. The last few times he hunted like that, the minute he snapped the light on, every one of them deer would close one eye."

Rufe Collins, still grinning from the encounter with Lizzie Gardner, said, "Old Harry really put his foot in it the time he came out of the woods and met Cal Dyer for the first time. Cal said to him, 'How's the hunting?' and Harry said, 'Not bad at all, I killed three deer before breakfast.' Cal asked, 'Do you know who I am?' Harry replied, 'No.' Cal said, 'I'm the new game warden for all of Waldo County!' Harry asked, 'Do you know who I am?' Cal said, 'No.' Harry said, 'I'm the biggest liar in the whole State of Maine!' "

Stan Pinkham added, "Harry used to brag about that coon hound he called Virgil. Claimed he didn't even have to go into the woods himself, all he had to do was take a board which he used to stretch coon pelts while they were drying, show Virgil the board, and he would take off into the woods and later he'd bring back a coon of just the right size to fit the board, exactly. One day his wife had asked him to fix her ironing board, so he came out of the house with it, headed for his workshop, and, without thinking, he walked by Virgil. That dog took one

look at that ironing board, headed for the woods, and no one has seen him since."

Ira said, "Harry once told me he was down on the shore, looking for poles to fix his pig pen and there was a feller from Rhode Island in a duck blind. A mallard made a pass over his tollers, he shot it, and as soon as the duck hit the water the hunter sent his dog out to get it. The funny part of it was that the dog walked out on the water, picked up the duck, and walked back to the blind. A little while later the same thing happened again, with the dog walking on the water. Harry was talking to the hunter but he did not comment on his unusual retriever, so finally the hunter asked Harry, 'Don't you notice anything unusual about my dog?' Harry said, 'Yes, poor thing can't swim.' "

All this time Uriah Boardman had been sitting by the stove reading the newspaper, alternately chuckling and grumbling over the articles.

"I just don't know what this world is coming to," he said in disgust. "According to this crime report, a car is stolen in Boston every 22 minutes. Why, in the name of common sense, don't they take it and hide it somewhere?"

Uriah is always unreasonable at the very mention of Boston. He took a trip down there a few years ago to visit his daughter and it was an experience that he never forgot. He was just sitting there on the train, minding his own business, when the conductor came along and said to him, "You can't leave that suitcase in the aisle," and continued on his rounds. Later he came back and said, "I told you, you can't leave that suitcase there, it's blocking the aisle," and went on his way again. On his next trip through Uriah's car he yelled, "I warned you not to leave that suitcase there!" He picked it up and threw it right out the door, then he looked at Uriah and said, "There! How do you like that?" Uriah looked him right in the face and eyes and said, "I wouldn't, if it was mine."

His daughter was living on the top floor of a hotel, 37 stories high, and of course Uriah had never seen a building that big before. He said he was so high up that a man wanted to commit suicide by jumping off the roof and he starved to death before he hit the sidewalk. Another man died in the night and they were so high up that they had to bring him down two flights to get him into heaven.

One morning he went down to the lobby to buy a newspaper. They had a big rack of papers from all over the world there, but he couldn't find what he wanted, so he

UP
DOWN

asked the clerk for a Belfast Journal. The clerk said, "Belfast? I don't even know where Belfast is." Uriah said, "If I was you, I wouldn't admit it, everyone in Belfast knows where Boston is."

We all get a good laugh out of his recounting of his experiences in the big city, but what happened to Fred Coombs was even worse. He was in Boston on business and he no sooner got there than a blizzard struck that was one of the worst in history. The city of Boston was closed tight with him without a place to sleep or a way to get out. He went to the Haymarket Hotel and asked for a room. The clerk said he was full up, but under the circumstances he would try and find him a cot to sleep on until the storm died out. Having nothing to do in the meantime, Fred went into the dining room to get something to eat and wait for the desk clerk to call him.

When the waiter came around, he suggested Fred try the house specialty, Boston Clam Chowder. Fred simply said, "I'll have a hamburger." The waiter said, "Don't you like clam chowder?" Fred said, "I like it, but don't want it. Bring me a hamburger." A few minutes later the head waiter came to Fred's table and asked, "What's wrong with the clam chowder? Don't you know that people come from all over the country for our clam chowder?" Fred, just a mite peeved, said, "If I can't get what I want here, I'll go somewhere else." A few minutes later he got his hamburger. After lunch, he wandered over to the desk to see if anything had turned up in the way of a room, and the clerk said, "You are in luck. We had an old man living on the tenth floor, and he just died. As soon as they get his room cleaned out, it's all yours."

Late that night, Fred was in bed just about to doze off

when a lady in white came into the room and walked right over to his bed, and without even turning the lights on, pulled the covers off him, rolled him over, and gave him a hypodermic, right where it hurts most. Come to find out, she was taking care of the old man, and nobody had told her of his passing.

Well, if you should mention the Haymarket Hotel to Fred he will warn you, "Whatever you do, don't refuse their clam chowder!"

After just a moment's thought, Stan Pinkham observed, "I just don't see any reason for traveling when we are already here."

"Say, Ira," I asked, "how cold was it out to your place this morning?"

"Only three degrees below zero at 6 a.m. Must be warming up some, days are getting longer now, and yesterday it was eight degrees below. Still cold enough to freeze two dry rags together. You know, every time I see the temperature drop below zero, I'd like to have one of them summer complaints here to see it. They are always telling us what a beautiful State we live in. God's country, they call it. Well, it may be God's country to them, but He sure don't spend his winters here."

"I'm glad I didn't live back in the real old days," I added. "Heard my Great Uncle Curt say that in those days it was a common sight after a snowstorm to see a man out poking around with a pole trying to find his chimney. He always said the only way to get out of the house was through the attic window on snowshoes. That was back when I was a boy and I used to wonder, with all that snow, what was the point of leaving the house at all?

"I remember one time listening to him tell some summer people about the time he was picking blueberries, and, all of a sudden, a great big bear stood right up in front of him and let out a helluva growl. Curt said he began to run, and the bear was hot on his heels. Well, they ran that way for quite some distance, and, finally, Curt said, the only way he could get clear of that bear was to run across Round Pond. It had just frozen over thick enough to support his weight, but the bear, being much heavier, broke through the ice and Curt got away.

"About that time, one of the summer people said, 'Now wait just a minute. You were picking blueberries when the chase started — that had to be in August, then you ran across a frozen pond? Now, I know Maine is famous for its unpredictable weather, but that's pretty hard to swallow!'

"Uncle Curt, pleased with himself that he had snared another victim, said, 'Oh, I just forgot to tell you that the bear chased me from August to Christmas!' "

"I outsmarted a bear one time" said Rufe Collins. "Bought a camp up on Mopang Stream from a guy down in New Jersey. Every spring he would go in there and

find the camp door stove in and all his provisions eaten or strewn around the floor. I guess he tried about everything for animal repellents but nothing worked, so after about four years of this he gave it up and sold the camp to me. Being from the city and all, he didn't know a thing about bear behavior so he just figured it was a lost cause and left Maine for good. Some years ago, I read an article in *Field & Stream* about bears, and it said that each bear will stake out a territory for itself and mark the boundary lines by clawing the bark off a big tree as high up the trunk as it can reach with its front paws. If another bear comes along, it will try to reach higher to make its mark, but if it can't reach above the first bear's marks it knows there is a bigger bear in the area, so it moves on to scout new territory. However, if the second bear can reach higher, it makes its marks above those of the first bear, and when the first bear comes by again he knows that a bigger bear has moved in, so he goes looking for another place.

"Armed with this knowledge, I simply took a stepladder and a garden rake, found the bear's marker tree, stepped up on the ladder, reached as high as I could, a

good 10 feet above the bear's marks, and dug some claw marks in the tree with the rake. To this day no one has seen a bear within 30 miles of my camp!"

While we were all sitting around trying to think up a new way to express our doubt, Ira said, "My father worked in a lumber camp down in that country back around 1898. He used to tell about two lumberjacks who were working side by side limbing two fallen trees. The trees were about 10 feet apart and they were each walking along on top of the trunks cutting off the limbs with very sharp axes. Suddenly, the head of one axe flew off, sailed through the air, and hit the other man right in the neck. Cut his head off as clean as a slice of bologna. 'Course, it was in the winter and there was snow on the ground, so they just stuck his head back on and packed his neck all around with snow. He had lost very little blood and he felt fine, so they went back to work.

"Come supper time they knocked off, and went into the cook shack for a feed of beans and biscuits. It was quite warm in the dining hall and the snow began to melt while the man ate his meal. On top of that, he had put a lot of pepper on his beans, and by and by he sneezed. His head flew off, rolled across the camp floor and fetched up against the stove leg and killed him deader than a pump handle."

"Strange things happen in lumber camps," said Uriah. "I worked in one myself the winter of '21 and '22. Always thought that digging clams was the worst kind of brutal amusement, so I tried my hand at chopping down trees. One winter of that was enough to drive me back to the coast. It was just my luck to get a camp where the foreman hated everyone. They say he wouldn't hire a

AH CHOO
GEZUNDHITE

man if he didn't like the way he combed his hair or took some other dislike to him. His name was Otis Cumerford, but we all called him Mr. Cumbersome — behind his back, of course. Anyway, one time this young feller came sauntering into camp just at sun-up before the day's work began, and he told Mr. Cumbersome that he wanted a job. Well, the boss didn't like the look of him, he was young for one thing, and he wasn't very big, either. I don't think he weighed more than a straw hat. Boss said, 'You don't look like a lumberjack to me, but take this axe and let me see you fell a tree.'

"Well sir, that kid took that axe and dropped a tree with one cut! The boss stood there with his eyes bugged out for a minute, and when he recovered he said, 'I'm impressed, yes, sir, but I thought I knew all the top-notch men in these woods. Say, where did you work last?' The young feller said, 'In the Sahara Forest.' Boss Cumerford asked, 'You mean Sahara Desert, don't you?' The kid replied, 'Well, it is now.'

"I was only in that camp that one winter, and that was enough for me," he continued. "Hard work from sun-up to sunset. We got enough to eat, but it was mostly stuff no one liked. In fact, someone asked the owner of the operation how he could afford to feed such a large crew of men and he said, 'That's simple: I find out what they don't like and give them plenty of it.'

"The owner's name was Eben Mactavish, an old country Scot, closer than the next minute with a dollar, and to see money wasted was the biggest aggrevation he could imagine. The old goat was always raving about the cost of equipment and finding fault with the men for misusing it. It wouldn't have been quite so bad if he'd stayed in Bangor where he belonged, but he was so afraid he might miss out on something to complain about that he was always hanging around watching the operation. There was a big log drive that year, and on three different occasions men were walking the logs, keeping them clear of snags in the river and, as will happen, they slipped and fell in. Every time this happened old Eben was right there watching, and the minute a man went into the water he'd hollar, 'Save his peavey!' He couldn't care less about the man, but them peavies cost $2.50 each and were harder to come by than a log driver. No one dared point out to him that most people considered a human life to be more valuable than a peavey, so they just put up with it. No unions in them days to protest, you know.

"Anyway, this went on until one day old Eben, thinking to get a better view of the drive, was up on a high bluff overlooking the river, standing up in the back of his car. It was a Maxwell touring car with the top down so he could see everything that was going on. His hired driver had the thing backed right up to the edge of the bluff, but old Eben kept yelling at him to back up a little more. Finally, after Eben swore at him to get closer, the hired driver slammed her into reverse and she lunged backwards, dropped over the edge, and the whole shooting match landed in the river! Without batting an eye, the drive boss yelled, 'Save his peavey!'

"I guess the only fun part of woods camp work is in the evening when each man, in turn, would sit on the 'Deacon's Seat' and tell stories. One of the stories I remember best was one told by John Dodge, a fellar from over to St. John, New Brunswick.

"Claimed he was fishing one time and caught a trout. After he was all done for the day, he gathered up all the fish he'd caught except one which had not died during the day, and when he went to reach for it, that fish stood up on its flippers and backed away from him. Being unable to catch the thing, he decided to give it up for a lost cause, and he started for the camp, walking up the tote road. He'd only gone about 100 yards when he heard a strange sound behind him. Turning around to see what it was, he was some surprised to see that trout following him home. The next day he came out of the camp and there was that fish rolling around in the pine needles and looking like he was having a gay old time. Every time John went to the woodpile or the privey, there was that fish following him just like a dog.

"After awhile, he got to where he would come right into the camp and he finally wound up sleeping on a wet rag by the woodbox. This went on all summer till one day John decided to go fishing again. He gathered up his fishing gear, and headed for the brook. Now, there was a footbridge over the brook, and he wanted to cross over because his fishing spot was on the other side. Well, he crossed over with that fish flopping along just behind him. They got about half-way across, where there was a wide crack in the boards, and John stepped over it, but that fish fell through, landed in the water, and drowned!"

Picking up my can of tobacco and heading for the door, I said to them, "That's it, I've got work to do, and the day is half gone showing no profit at all."

The old car started, after considerable effort, and I headed for home, pondering over whether or not I should have a hand choke installed as Junior had suggested. I still think it would be cheaper to quit smoking.

I saw a robin this morning, on my way out to the woodpile. I was just looking around like you do in the early spring, and if flew right past my head. About 4 p.m. I was sitting on the piazza enjoying the sun and watching the snow melt when the mailman pulled up out front and stuffed something into my mailbox. My box is the last one on his route, so he was sitting in his car, lighting his pipe, and getting ready to call it a day.

"Afternoon, Asa," I said, "got time for a glass of mulled cider?"

"No, thanks, Ken," he says, "but I might have a cup of coffee if you have one kicking around."

"Sure thing, come up on the piazza and make yourself at home," I told him.

There are few things in life that give a man more pleasure than sitting on a piazza in the spring sunshine with a good cup of coffee and an old friend to swap a few yarns with.

Asa's mind was on a different tack, however, and he sat back in the old rocker and said, "I was just thinking about the last time I took a drink of hard stuff. It was just 28 years ago this spring. In those days I was building boats and, on occasion, coffins, too. Early one morning the undertaker, Wallace Mallett, came to me and said, 'Asa, I've got to have a coffin by tomorrow night.'

" 'Gorry, Wallace,' I said, 'It's awful short notice, ain't it?' And he said, 'Well, how much notice can you expect on such a job? Seriously now, I know it's a lot of work in a short time, so I brought you a jug of Old Melody to help the job along.'

"Well," Asa continued, "I was just finishing a cat boat for Joe Fisher's son, so as soon as the tiller was set in place I went to work on that coffin. I didn't spare myself any, and I didn't spare that Old Melody, either. I worked on it all night and it was finished just as the jug was finished, just before daylight. The next day, around

noon, Wallace came to the door and asked if the coffin was ready. We walked out to the workshop, I opened the door, and I noticed that Wallace had a funny look on his face. I looked in and there was that coffin, and she had a rudder and a centerboard on her!

" 'Godfry Mighty,' he said, 'Do me a favor, will you? When I kick the bucket, make sure someone else builds my coffin. I don't want to sail into the great beyond looking like I'm not taking it seriously!' "

Looking down the road towards town, watching the snow melt and form little rivers that merged and became fair-sized streams in the deep ditches on both sides of the road, I was thinking of the old days when all the roads were dirt and spring was called mud season. After a winter of uncommonly deep snow the roads were impassable quagmires for a couple of months. Out loud I remarked, "It was the spring of 1933 as I recall, I was standing on this very spot, and suddenly, I spotted an object working its way up the road. Couldn't figure out what it was, it was about the size of a cat, but cats don't walk in the mud if they can help it, and I knew it wasn't a woodchuck — too early for them. Besides, a woodchuck would be moving along the stone wall, not in the middle of the road like that.

"About two hours later it came up even with the house, here, and I could see that it was a hat. Yessir, a brown Fedora hat. Well, I thought I recognized it, so I walked over to it, and when I got close enough I could see it was old John Prince.

" 'Kinda muddy walking ain't it, John?' I asked. And you know what he said?

" 'Oh hell, I ain't afoot, I'm on horseback!' "

Asa added, "I don't remember that, but I do recall that old John was probably the most stubborn man that ever lived. I told him one time, 'John,' I said, 'you are so stubborn and contrary, if you ever fell in the river and drowned, we'd look for your body upstream.' "

Asa continued, "In fact, he was so pigheaded people used to make up stories about him. I heard one time that it came suppertime and old John was nowhere to be found. They checked the barn, woodpile, and the privey but he was nowhere about, so they sent his grandson, Willie, out to find him. Willie looked everywhere and kept getting further away from the house. Finally, he looked up and there was old John standing in a thicket out back of the woodlot. Willie told him supper was ready, and trotted back to the house. They all sat down to eat and old John still didn't show up, so Willie was sent out again to see what was keeping him. Willie found old John still standing in the same spot, so he asked if he was coming to supper. Old John said, 'Nope.' Willie said, 'Why not, Gramp?' Old John said, 'I'm standing in a bear trap.' "

"Old John had a way with words, alright," I said. "They claim that when he got married he was bringing his new bride home in the wagon and for some reason the horse stumbled. John said, 'That's once.' A few hundred yards down the road the horse stumbled again. John said, 'That's twice.' Before they got home the horse stumbled again, and John said, 'That's three times!' Then he took a rifle out from under the seat and shot that horse dead. Well, of course, his new bride was shocked and surprised at this unexpected behavior, so she laid into him. Called him everything she could lay her tongue to, and really laid him out in lavender. When

she finally ran down, he just looked her right cold stone in the eye and said, 'That's once.' From that day on they never had a difference of opinion on anything."

"You know," said Asa, "that's one of the things that people from away can't seem to figure out about Maine people. We do tend to be brief in our speech. Old John was a man of few words, as they say. Far as I'm concerned, I don't see any point in continuing to talk when you've said your piece. Anything I can't abide is someone who keeps talking long after he's made his point."

"Sometimes a few words is all that's necessary," I said. "Last summer I was talking to a fella from Connecticut, and he was telling me about the time he ran into a really strange character up in Lincoln. Seems he had this hunting camp out in the woods up there and one winter there was a much heavier snowfall than usual, so he came up on a weekend to shovel off the roof so it wouldn't cave in. Well, he drove in as far as he could, then he started walking. Just as he crossed a brook he noticed a little boy skating on the ice, and while he was watching, the boy fell in and went right under the ice. Of course, he beat it right down there and grabbed the kid by the collar and pulled him out onto the bank. He asked the boy where he lived and he said, 'Just a little way, if I cut through the woods.' Well, the boy went on home and the fella walked in to his camp, started the fire and poured himself a stiff drink. While he was sitting in front of the fire, thinking about what a close call that boy had had, he heard a knock on the door, and when he opened it, there was this middle-aged woman standing there. She asked, 'Are you the man who pulled my little boy out of the brook?' The feller said, 'Yes, I am.' She said, 'You didn't happen to see what be-

came of his mittens, did you?' "

Lighting his pipe again, Asa added, "I'm reminded of that family of summer people who own that big place out on Duck Cove. A few years ago they all arrived here for the summer, and that oldest daughter of theirs, Jayne, I think her name was, seems she had a boyfriend back in New York City, and she was some put out being forced to spend all summer in Marshall's Landing without him. Anyway, she was walking around all huffy and feeling hateful, finally walked right up to Edgar Wood and said, 'Say, what do you do for excitement around here anyway?' Edgar just looked her in the eye and said, 'I wouldn't know. I've never been excited.'

"I understand," said Asa, "that before the summer was gone she took up with one of Willis Gilbert's boys, and her parents had the devil's own works dragging her back to New York. She ended up getting married to the boy in New York, but at least she don't hate Maine anymore."

"I remember my father telling me about old Mrs.

Prindall years ago," I said. "She and her husband owned that old mansion out on Clam Point, the one that burned down about 20 years ago. They owned a soap factory in New Jersey and they had enough money to burn a wet elephant. Anyway, the last anyone saw of them was the time she came to the mansion right after her husband died. It was left to her to clean the place out and put it up for sale.

"The day she arrived she put up a notice on the bulletin board in front of the old town hall, that she wanted to hire a driver for the summer. Most of the men in town were either busy with building lobster traps, or something, so she wound up hiring Cliff King. Well, it seems the more money some folks have the more they like to lord it over the rustics in a place like this. But, on the other hand, Cliff's ancestors settled in Maine at least 150 years ago, so he wasn't the type to take any guff from outsiders.

"As I say, Cliff took the job and Mrs. Prindall told him that his first duty would be to pick her up at the mansion — the cottage, she always called it — and drive her into town.

"Next morning, bright and early, Cliff was sitting in the wagon at the front door of the 'cottage,' and out comes Mrs. Prindall all dolled up to impress the town folks. As she stepped into the wagon, Cliff remarked, 'It's a fine day for a drive, isn't it?' She just plopped herself down in the back seat and said, 'Mr. King, I hired you to drive my wagon, not socialize with your employer!' Apparently Cliff's motto was 'Don't get mad, get even,' 'cause he never spoke a word to her all summer. At the end of the season he handed her an itemized bill for his services, and as she was reading it over she came to an item she didn't understand, so she said to him, 'What is this item here for five dollars?' Cliff, adopting a real haughty air, said, 'That's for SASS — I don't often take it, and when I do, I charge.'

"I guess when money comes up against pride there's bound to be an explosion. She sold the mansion and never set foot in Marshall's Landing again."

"Speaking of money," Asa said, "I was in to Andy's Hardware store the other day, and we were discussing the economy and all, business has been poor lately, so he was complaining about lack of trade and the value of the dollar. I told him that money couldn't buy happiness, and he says, 'Money can't buy happiness, but if you've got enough of it, you get to choose the kind of misery that suits you best.' I guess prob'ly it has been tough for him lately. I was in there about two months ago and Andy was gone somewhere. I asked Keith, the stock boy, where Andy was and he said, 'He's up town buying more red ink.'

"One time last summer, one of them summer complaints came in to Andy's place. Said he wanted to buy two feet of stovepipe. Keith told him that it only came in four foot sections. Well, this bird insisted that he only wanted two feet of pipe, so Keith says, 'I'll go out back and ask Andy about it.' Keith went out back where Andy was taking inventory and said to him, 'Some fool wants to buy half a stovepipe,' and after he said it he noticed that the feller had followed him into the back room, and Keith said, 'and this gentleman wants to buy the other half.' "

A few minutes passed while Asa and I sat watching the snow melt and wondering if the coming summer would be any different from last. After awhile he asked, "How do you feel about the school board wanting to bring back corporal punishment? I hear the kids are getting pretty wild."

"It don't do any good to lick a kid," I answered, "Why, the worst licking I ever got was for telling the truth!"

Asa just looked at me and remarked, "Well, you got to admit it cured you."

"Don't forget," I said, "tomorrow is town meeting. One thing we have to decide is what we are going to do with our trash now that the government has ruled that town dumps have to go. Now ain't that something? Next thing you know we'll have to build a recreation center for the seagulls and rats, if we take the dump away from them."

"Yes," said Asa, "and we'll have to find another job for old Tom, the dump tender. He's not what you would call the brains of the outfit. Gonna be hard finding a job he can handle, poor soul."

"Why don't we get him to run for President?" I asked. "You remember when we were boys in school, they always told us that anyone could become President. Seems to me the last two or three of them have proved it."

When you live in Maine, there is a ritual which you must put up with every six months, called state inspection of motor vehicles. Every time you drive into an inspection station you just know that they are going to find something wrong, and declare your car a death trap. Of course, it's never anything that they can't fix for a price, and the older your car is, the more they find wrong with it, and the higher the price of the repairs. I've been to other states, such as Connecticut, where they have no such foolishness, and wondered why there were no more death traps on the road than here in Maine where they are inspected every six months.

Today, it was my turn to take my car in for a check-up. It's not new, and hasn't been for some years now.

As I drove into the inspection station I knew I was in trouble when Burt Doughty yelled: "Hey, anyone killed in that wreck?"

Usually the filling station is a loose and friendly place, but at inspection time it becomes a dreadful part of an expensive ordeal. A visit to the dentist is no picnic, but a man's pocket nerve is even more sensitive. When you get between a Mainer and his wallet, you are on thin ice.

While Burt jacked up my car to check ball joints, muffler, and all the other expensive parts, I went into his office to visit with the local characters who always hang out around there. I knew my car would get a good going-over because Tim Hanson of the state police was there. He was telling the others about something that happened in court the other day, and I settled back in one of the filthy chairs to listen.

Tim continued: "I had warned him to get his brakes fixed about three months ago but he didn't bother, so a few days ago I come up behind him out on the old mill road. He was wandering back and forth across the road, and when we came to that sharp curve by the old granite quarry he slowed down some, but I noticed that his brake lights didn't come on, so I knew he was still driving with no brakes, and I stopped him. I asked him why he didn't get his brakes fixed and he said, 'Hell, I have a hard enough time getting this heap started, let alone getting it stopped!'

"Anyway," Tim went on, "I had to pinch him that time, so, after Judge Coffin heard his case, he was fined $25. As he was paying the fine he asked the Judge for a receipt, and the Judge said to him, 'Sure you can have a receipt, but what's the matter, don't you trust me?'

"The old feller looked the judge right in the eye and said, 'Oh, sure, I trust you, but you and I are getting along in years now, and before too long we are both going to be meeting our maker. Well, when I get to the pearly gates, Saint Peter is going to ask me if I've ever committed a crime and I'll have to say "Yes." He's going to ask if I've ever been to court, and I'll have to say "Ayuh." Then he will ask if I paid my fine, and Judge, if I don't have the receipt, they are going to be looking all over Hell for Judge Coffin!'

"Judges usually have the last word, but not that time," said Tim.

By this time Burt had finished his inspection and was standing in the doorway. When he asked for my registration I knew he had not found anything wrong with my car, this time. While he was filling out the sticker for the windshield he said to Tim: "What's this I hear about that cop up in Portland quitting the force?"

Tim answered, "Yes — the way I hear it, it all goes back to when Maine outlawed aerosol cans last year. This city cop came into the police station the other day with his uniform all torn up, hat missing, and his badge in his hand. He walked into the chief's office, threw the badge on the desk and said: 'I quit.'

"The chief asked what happened and the officer said: 'It's these environmentalists — I just got beat up trying to make an arrest.' The chief asked, 'Why blame it on the environmentalists?' The cop said, 'People just won't stand for us using roll-on mace!' "

"Yessir," Tim went on, "you know, most people don't think of a courtroom as being very funny, but some strange things happen there. You must have heard that old Will Seavey finally got caught for poaching deer? Why, that old goat has been a poacher longer than anyone can remember — one of the all-time greats, you might say. Anyway, it seems he was coming out of the woods with his gun on one shoulder and a small deer on the other, but he wasn't paying too much attention and he walked right out in the face of the game warden. You fellers probably don't know him — a young feller from up around Portland. Everyone says he's scared to go in the woods so he just rides around checking licenses as the hunters are coming out to their cars. I guess he does get out of his car once in awhile this time of year, checking beaver dams and so forth. I know he wasn't expecting to run into a poacher this time of year, so he and Will were both somewhat surprised to meet under the circumstances. The warden was just standing there by the side of the road when Will stepped out of the woods lugging that deer and rifle. 'Well, what do you think you're doing?' the warden asked. And Will said, 'Oh nothing, just croosing.' Then the warden said, 'Croosing? What do you call that on your shoulder?' Old Will looked around and says, 'That's my rifle.' The warden said, 'No, I mean on your *other* shoulder!' Old Will looked the other way, jumped back, and yelled, 'Yikes! Where the hell did that come from!?'

"'Course, even the greenest warden in the state wouldn't buy that, so he pinched him and took the deer and Will's rifle. In fact, it was the same rifle his father took after the thief with that time the old man caught him coming out of the coop with a Rhode Island Red under his arm. He yelled at him to stop or die where he stood. The thief stopped, looked around at the old man, and just laughed. He said, 'You're so old, you can barely stand up, let alone hit anything with that thing!' The old man hauled up, drew a bead, and took that hen's head off just like that!" Tim snapped his fingers loudly. "Well, say, that thief dropped that chicken and beat it some quick. There was a lot of that sort of thing going on during the Depression, what with so many hungry tramps traveling around the country. They say that from that day on, they never had another tramp anywhere near the place.

"Anyway, Old Will wasn't too shook up about being caught, but he was real concerned about turning that rifle over to the state. Well, as I say, he made his appearance in court, pleaded guilty, and the judge fined him $200. As he was paying his fine, in cash, this warden had to rub it in a little, and he said, 'That's pretty expensive deer meat, isn't it, Will?'

"Old Will just glanced at him sideways, kept counting, and said, 'I figure over a period of 40 years, about 2¢ a pound!'

"I was surprised that the Judge fined him so much. Usually, these days, they either just slap them on the wrist or they jump on the arresting officer for failing to say 'May I' when he made the pinch. It's more like the old days when I first got into law enforcement. My first

case was the town drunk up in West Athens. The judge fined him $30 for being drunk in public, and the old drunk says to the judge, 'Can't pay it. You can't blood out of a turnip!'

"That judge gave him a look that would wilt a fence post and said: 'Quite so, but we can keep the turnip — 30 days!' "

I was about to leave when Doctor Payne drove in to fill up that gas-guzzling pleasure-palace he calls a car. I heard Burt tell him to turn his engine off 'cause it burns gas faster than he could pump it into the tank.

None of us ever could figure out why a man with a name like Payne decided to become a doctor. We have ribbed him about that for years, but he just grins and keeps on making huge deposits at the bank. Being a doctor of dentistry makes it even worse, but no matter how much we ride him about it he's always been good natured. Maybe it's because he knows that sooner or later he will get his revenge on every one of us.

As he came into the station to pay for the gas, I said to him, as I always do, "How's business, Doc?"

And he answered, as usual, "Oh, I just keep grinding away." If he ever thought up a new answer, we would probably wonder if he was sick.

While Burt was filling his cash register with the doctor's money he asked, "Did you ever get them false teeth of Maynard Calderwood's to fit? He's been complaining about them for a month or more now."

Doc replied, "I've had the devil's own works making him a set of choppers. His face is bent from that time the horse kicked him, you know. 'Course he won't admit it, so he lays it to my incompetence, but his jaw is shaped like a fox trap that a moose stepped on, but I'm doing the best I can. The first time he came in to be fitted I sent him away knowing he'd be back, and sure enough, a week later there he was again saying they hurt his mouth. Well, I ground them down here and there and off he went again. A week later he was back, said they hurt the other side of his mouth this time. I worked them over again, and a few days later he was back again. I said to him, 'For Pete's sake, are those teeth still hurting you?'

"You know what the old coot said to me? He said, 'Well, I'll tell you, Doc. The old lady and me was out fishing the other day, and she hooked a big salmon. Had an awful time reeling it in, and when she got it right alongside the boat, I bent over to gaff it, slipped, fell across the gunnel, and the oar lock caught me in the groin, and for about half an hour, them teeth didn't bother me a bit!' "

Doc Payne has a son working for a newspaper up in Portland, and when I asked how the boy was doing, Doc grinned and started telling us about the letter he got from him a few days ago. Seems that one day things were a little slack so the editor sent the boy out to one of the nursing homes to try and get a human interest story for the paper.

When he got there and looked around, he singled out an old man for the interview. Asked him about his life, what he had done for work and all, any vices he might have had, and finally, he asked the old man to what did he attribute his long life. The old feller told him all about his life, said he had worked as a lumberjack most of his years, then he told the boy that he figured he had lived a long time because he had worked hard all his life, had never tasted any kind of alcohol, only had one woman in his whole life, and his next birthday would be his 87th.

Being a typical Mainer, the old timer had been quite brief in the telling of his story, so the boy hunted up another resident, figuring to do one more interview to make the trip worthwhile.

The second old feller told a somewhat different story. Claimed that he had only worked when he had to, and not too hard at that, dug a few clams in the summer, raked a few blueberries, cut pulpwood until winter really set in, then he didn't do much of anything until spring when the clam flats thawed out again. When asked about vices, the old feller said he drank a little now and then, chased a few women, that is, up until recent years when he forgot why he was chasing them. He couldn't seem to believe it was simply due to old age, said it was that stuff they put in his food back during World War I. He couldn't remember what they called it, but said it started to work when he was about 80. Anyway, when he was asked why he thought he had lived so long he said it was simply due to moderation in all things, and when asked his age he said he was almost 94.

Wanting to make sure he had enough material for a

whole newspaper article, Doc's boy decided to do one more interview, so he looked all around and finally settled on this old codger sitting in a wheelchair with a shawl around his shoulders, all bent over, with more wrinkles than last year's crab apple.

The boy asked him the same questions, but he was some surprised at the answers he got this time. That old feller told him that he had never done an honest, full day's work in his life, he had drunk enough booze to float a battleship, smoked four packs of cigarettes a day for years, chased more women than a computer could count, and otherwise had just raised hell all his life. Stunned by all this the boy finally asked him how old he was and the feller said, "If I live until November 5th, I'll be 46."

I've always had a lot of affection and respect for old people. They have lived in times that the rest of us only read about. They can tell you details that most history books don't bother with, and details can often make history more interesting. If you can talk to someone who remembers the past, they can often give you information which is just as accurate and even more interesting than the facts and dates in history books. I always figured it was because there is nothing human about facts and dates. Many old people also have a great sense of humor, as that young reporter found out when he did that last interview.

Now that summer is here, there are two things we have to deal with: crabgrass, and summer complaints. I don't know what it is with lawnmowers, but they seem to winter-kill. You leave one sitting in the shed all winter and when you want to use it the following year, it just squats there making sputtering sounds. Sometimes it will yank the pull-cord out of your hand as if it resents being called on to go to work. I yanked and fiddled with my mower for most of an hour before giving it up. Years ago folks used to cut grass with a scythe, and the lazy ones kept goats. This fool machine probably don't know it, but it's in danger of being replaced by a living creature. That would be a switch, wouldn't it?

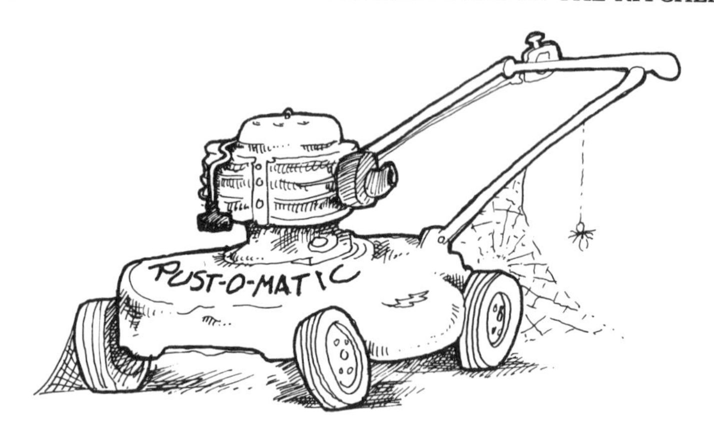

Oh, well, it was too nice a day to be spoiled by a piece of junk, so I decided to walk to the hardware store knowing full well that Andy wouldn't have a scythe in stock, but also knowing the walk would do me good. As I approached that big pine tree that marks the property line between my land and Joel Hooper's, I could see him there, and as I drew near I could see that he was fixing the fence where a limb had fallen and broke the wire. One nice thing about walking, when you see someone you know, you stop and talk. If you are in a car you just wave and keep on going, never knowing what you missed by being in a hurry.

"Morning, Joel," I said. "You're right on the job today. That limb just fell last night, I know 'cause it was still stuck to the tree when I went by yesterday afternoon."

"Yes," he says, "but them cows of mine hang around this tree for shade when it's hot and I don't want them to get out of the pasture and be wandering around in the road now that the summer complaints are around. You remember that three years ago my best Jersey got out, started across the road, and got run over by a summer complaint. Anyone has got to be pretty numb to hit a cow with a car. Killed her, of course, and then he didn't want to pay for her, so I had him hauled into court. Lucky for me that old Oscar Tibbetts saw the whole thing. Oscar said that car must have been doing 80 down that road. That feller got himself a high-priced lawyer from Boston, but he couldn't shake Oscar a bit. He asked Oscar, 'What's your name?' Oscar answered, 'Oscar Tibbetts.' The lawyer asked, 'Where do you live?' 'Marshall's Landing,' replied Oscar. 'You lived here all your life?' Oscar said, 'Not yet!'

"That lawyer could see that he wasn't going to shake Oscar, so he advised his client to pay for the cow."

"Reminds me of the time old Tom, the dump tender, lost his cow," I said. "He wasn't much for mending fences, and she got out of the pasture, started across the railroad track and a *Bangor & Aroostook* freight train caught her broadside and killed her deader than a door nail. Couple of days later this agent from the main office went to see Tom in person about a settlement. He says how sorry he is about the unfortunate accident and all, told Tom he figured the settlement should be about $50. Tom agreed, and that was that. 'Bout a week later the agent was back with a voucher for Tom to sign, and Tom asks what that voucher thing is and what's it for. The agent says he has to sign it to settle the claim, so Tom was about to make his mark when the agent says that they had been talking it over at the main office, and they decided that this accident was worth $75. Old Tom pushed the voucher back at that agent and allowed, 'Not by a damn sight — we agreed on $50, and I ain't payin' a cent more!' Old Tom always claimed that he would not have ended up as dump tender if his dairy herd hadn't been wiped out."

"Yessir," said Joel, "this old pine tree has shaded a good many cows in its lifetime, but if the limbs keep falling off I guess they'll just have to find another shady spot. You know, I had a herd of Holsteins years ago, 'bout all they knew enough to do was give a lot of milk. Not half as smart as these Jerseys of mine. I remember one time we had a dry spell that lasted three months. Not a drop of rain, hotter than the hinges of Tofit, temperature in the 90's every day. At that time I had me a corn field right next to the pasture, and one day it was so hot that the corn got overheated, started popping, and in no time the air was full of popcorn. Well, sir, as I say, them Holsteins was so stupid, they saw that popcorn coming down, thought it was snow and everyone of them fool cows stood there and froze to death."

'Course, I didn't let on that I didn't believe him. Someday he's apt to tell the truth, by accident, and I wouldn't want him to see any change in my reaction. I've known him for 40 years now, and I'm still waiting.

After lighting my pipe and taking my time about it, I said to Joel, "You know, my Uncle Curt told me that he had a herd of cows years ago, Holsteins they was, too. Probably during that same dry spell. According to him it was so dry, so long, that every cow in the country dried up except his. Claimed that just before the worst of the drought hit, he had all his cows fitted with green sunglasses, and them cows, stupid Holsteins like you say, they didn't know that the grass they were eating was all dead and brown. They kept right on giving milk as usual, but one morning some kids got into his pasture and stole every pair of them sunglasses. The next day his cows had dried up just like everyone else's."

"You talk about dry spells," said Joel, "one time my well water was starting to taste real funny, so I put some in a bottle and sent it up to Augusta for testing. A few days later this feller showed up, said he was an engineer of some kind, looked my farm all over, paid special attention to the well, and finally he says to me, 'Your cesspool is too close to your well. Now, you have to make a decision here, either stop using the well, or stop using the cesspool.'

"At that time we still had the old out-house, so I figured we could get along without the cesspool, but we couldn't get along without the well. We quit using the cesspool, and three days later the well dried up."

"That's a sample of the good old days folks keep talking about," I remarked. "I wish some of those people who keep talking about the 'good old days' could spend some time with my Uncle Curt. He remembers those times as they really were. He told me that when he was a boy, he was 16 years old before he got his first pair of shoes, and by then his feet were so tough he wore them out on the inside first.

"And talk about weather! He used to say that if the government ever set up a weather station in his backyard, they would have to re-write all the record books. According to him, they had a rainy spell that lasted so long there were three babies born with webbed feet and a man was drowned in a corn crib."

Joel's only comment was, "Would you just as soon pull that wire tight while I nail it?"

Pulling it as hard as I could, I mentioned that the post itself was loose, and Joel said, "Can't be helped, the dirt here is pretty thin, can't drive posts into bedrock. It's almost as bad as my garden. Soil is so thin I have to plant my seeds with a shotgun."

"Speaking of gardens," I said, "Uncle Curt claimed he made a scarecrow one time that scared the crows so bad, they brought back the corn they had stolen two years back."

That seemed to get Joel's mind off fence mending, and he said, "You remember Fred Collins, used to own that farm where the Johnson's live now? He came over one time, always bragging about his garden, says to me, 'Say, Joel, I was wondering if I could borrow your cross-cut saw? I've raised me some pumpkins that are so big, I'll have to cut them in half before I can put them in the wagon.' Now, I'll tell you, he backed off some quick when I says, 'Sure, you can have it, if you can get it. Right now it's down in my garden, pinched in a beet!'

"'Course I'd been laying for him ever since the time my whole potato crop blighted and I tried to buy some from him. I told him I only wanted about a hundred pounds for my own use. That old goat says, 'No — I don't think I'd sell any, I just don't want to cut any of mine in half.'"

While we were finishing the fence mending job, a big black Cadillac with New Jersey plates went by going like the hammers of Hades, and Joel remarked, "Guess we got the fence fixed just in time, the cow killers are back again.

"They can be a pain sometimes," he continued, "but some of them are fun to have around. Last summer, this tourist stopped while I was fixing this same fence, and we was just jawing about this and that. He wasn't in a hurry; in fact, he seemed quite interested in 'local life styles,' as he put it. Come to find out, he was a vice president of some big company in New York, and he'd never been to Maine before.

"One thing he wanted to know was where all these rocks came from. I told him as far as I know the glaciers brought them. He says 'Glaciers? What glaciers? Where are they?'

" 'Gone back for another load of rocks!' I told him.

"He was looking out across the pasture there, and he says, 'Can you tell me why that cow over there has no horns?'

"So I gave him a quick lecture on cows, told him there were many reasons why cows don't have horns, sometimes they get diseased and fall off, sometimes we have to cut them off so they don't hook each other, but, I says, the reason that particular animal doesn't have horns is because it's a horse.

"Another time I was plowing with my ox, the reason being that my hired man had run my tractor over a rock-pile and busted the transmission, and this summer complaint came along, wanted to know why I was plowing with a bull. He couldn't see the difference, I guess. I told him that I just wanted to let the bull know that life

around here is not all fun and games."

"That the same hired man who got your daughter in trouble?" I asked.

"Yes," he says, "Some clumsy, he was."

"I was just thinking of the time Uncle Curt and I were hauling a load of cow manure down to his lower field," I said. "Something let go on the wagon tongue and the whole load upset and spread itself all over the road. We were just standing there, wondering what to do next and this summer complaint pulled up, stopped, got out of the car, and looked it all over. Finally he says to me, 'Well fellers, looks like your wagon is ok, but there ain't much left of your cow.' "

"What tickles me," Joel added, "is, they think we are the odd ones.

"One other time there was a feller from Texas stopped to talk to me," Joel said. "He didn't stay long. Asked me how much land I was working, I told him 'bout 200 acres. He said, 'Nice little farm you got here, but back in Texas on my ranch it takes me all day to drive from one end of my property to the other.'

"All I said was, 'I know what you mean. I had a car like that once, myself.' He didn't stay long after that."

"Look, I've got to get going," I said, "almost forgot where I was headed."

"Come again," Joel said, and I started off to shop for that scythe.

When I arrived at the hardware store there was quite a group of people coming and going or just sitting on the bench out front. I got there just in time to hear Frank Rizzo trying to give Rufe Collins a hard time. Frank had moved here from Ohio a few years back and it has al-

ways bothered him that he has never been accepted as a native. I overheard him say to Rufe, "For Pete's sake, how long do I have to live here before you people stop calling me 'that feller from away'?"

Rufe replied, "Well, I'll tell you. Many years ago they was a feller who came here from New York with his parents. He was six months old when they moved here, and he grew up here, lived here all his life until he died at the age of 84. We all liked him a lot, so we had something special carved on his tombstone. It said, 'HE WAS ALMOST ONE OF US'."

Of course that didn't satisfy Frank at all so he said, "Look, I don't ever expect to be considered a native, but I've lived here for more than 20 years now. Three of my children were born here. Now, don't that make THEM natives?"

Rufe never does know when to let up and so he said, "No, not really. If your cat had kittens in the oven, you wouldn't call them biscuits, would you?"

Andy saw me coming and asked, "What can I do for you?"

"I want to buy a scythe," I replied.

"What do you want with a scythe?" he asked.

"It's cheaper than a herd of goats," I told him.

Apparently he decided not to pry any further, so he simply said, "I haven't had a scythe in stock for years. The Grim Reaper bought my last one 18 years ago."

There was a conversation going on over in the corner, and I caught just enough of it to wonder what it was all about. When I asked who was being raked over the coals this time, Jake Sawyer said, "I was just telling them about Sam Crawford. He turned 90 last week."

"Old Sam could say more in one sentence than most folks could say in a book," I said. "It used to run in his family, I always thought. Even them two nieces of his who used to live over on the crossroad. Remember them? Old maids, both of them. Scared to death of men. Even the milkman had to leave his deliveries out by the mail box 'cause they didn't dare let him anywhere near them. I can't imagine how they came to be so afraid of men, but they thought that all kinds of awful things would happen if they got near one. They even had an old female cat for a pet. Wouldn't let her out of the house either, for the same reason.

"Finally, one of them did wind up getting married, and went away on her honeymoon. A few days later the other one got a post-card from her and all it said was, 'Let the cat out.' "

I don't know how anyone can take care of more than one cow. We only have the one, don't need more than one for the family, but this one cow is more bother than anything I have. While I was milking this morning I heard a footstep behind me, looked up, and there was the Rev. Ernest Tarbox coming into the tie-up.

"Morning, Reverend," I said.

"Morning, Kendall," he replied. I figured he was making his monthly visit to give me hell for not going to church.

"I was just wondering if I could borrow your lawn mower?" he said.

"Sure, you can borrow it," I told him, "but it won't do you much good. Hasn't started since last September." I lied a little, and regretted it immediately. Always feel a little funny about lying to a preacher, but can't seem to stop. Besides, I figure they need a little something to work on, anyway. He knew I was stretching the truth, but he also knew it wasn't an out and out lie.

"Go ahead and take it. Maybe it will start for you," I said.

"Reminds me of that young preacher over to Stockton" he replied. "Seems he hadn't been there very long when he heard about two brothers who had not spoken to each other for 20 years. They had had a row about the ownership of a wheelbarrow, and never did get it settled. Anyway, this young preacher got wind of it and was talking to one of the brothers on the street. He said he thought it was a terrible thing that they had not spoken in 20 years, and he wanted to try to get them back on speaking terms if he could.

"The preacher allowed that he had a plan, and he told the brother that he was not a betting man but he figured that he was willing to bet five dollars that the next time this man saw his brother, and if he spoke first, his brother would answer and the feud would be ended.

"George, his name was, thought about it for a minute, and finally agreed.

"While they were talking, George's brother appeared on the scene, coming toward them. The preacher saw him coming so he said to George 'Here comes your brother now. Go ahead and speak to him and five dollars says he will answer.' George waited until his brother was close enough to see him and, just as his brother was about to cross the street to avoid him, he yelled 'Hey, brother, why don't you bring back my wheelbarrow, you damn thief!' Then he turned to the preacher and said, 'You lose.'

"Well," I said, "they say money talks."

"Yes," replied Reverend Tarbox, "but sometimes what it says is not for mixed company."

It was apparent that he was in a talking mood, so I just kept on with the milking and he started up again.

"I was just remembering my first day on the job when I came here 46 years ago this summer. It was right in the middle of the haying season, and when I got to the church there was only one sinner sitting there. The time to begin came and went. No one else showed up, so I asked that one old feller if I should give my sermon anyway. He was a typical Downeaster, couldn't give me a direct answer, and said to me, 'If I took a load of hay down to the pasture, and only one cow showed up, I'd feed her.' Taking that to mean that he wanted a sermon, I went to the pulpit and preached a two hour sermon just as if the church had been full. Well, as I say, that was my first public sermon, so I was wondering if it was alright. After I finished, I asked that old timer what he thought of my sermon, and he said, 'If I took a load of hay down to the pasture and only one cow showed up, I wouldn't give her the whole damn load!' "

"I suppose young preachers are just like anyone else, they make a few mistakes being new on the job and all," I said. "I'll never forget that young feller they sent here to fill in for you while you were on leave to Africa that time. He came from the city and really didn't know how to talk to country folks like us. He'd only been around for a week or two when he started finding fault with the church. Said it was too dark and not very classy. Well, he hit on an idea to brighten the place up and to give it some class at the same time. What he had in mind was to install a chandelier, one of them fancy expensive ones. When he made his announcement about what he wanted to do, he said he was going to pass a special plate around to take up a collection just for the chandelier. The plate came around and old Enoch Nickerson just sat there and let it go by without giving the 'extra dollar' the preacher asked for.

"After the sermon, the preacher was standing by the door thanking everyone for their donations, but when Enoch came by he just stood there looking at him. Enoch knew the preacher was watching him during the collection, so he said 'I didn't put an extra dollar in the special plate, and I've got three good reasons why. One, I didn't have a "extra dollar," never had an "extra dollar." Two, you want to buy one of them chandelier things, and there ain't a soul in this town who knows how to play one, and three, if you want to brighten up the church, why don't you do something about the damn lights?'

"While we are on preacher stories, I was wondering if you ever heard of that old-time preacher who was asked to pray for rain?" I asked the Reverend.

He just stood there looking puzzled, and finally he said "No, I don't know as I ever did. What about him?"

"It seems," I began, "that down in Oxford County there was an old minister who had been at it for years, and, after a long spell of hot, dry weather the folks in his congregation were really up against it. Cows dried up, crops failed, wells went dry and all that. Matter of fact they had a funeral and they had to prime the mourners. Anyway, this dry spell became quite a worry to those people, so, one Sunday the minister was handed a note during his sermon. After he finished his sermon he announced that he had been requested to pray for rain. The old feller looked out the window at the weather vane on top of the nearest barn and said, 'I'd be happy to pray for rain, but I can tell you right now, it won't do a bit of good unless that wind changes.'"

"Sounds like he was more practical than faithful," replied the Reverend. "Reminds me of them two lobster fishermen down to Rockland. They was more faithful than practical. Seems they were out hauling their traps when a storm came out of nowhere. Raining like the heavens had opened up, wind blowing a living judgement. She started to take on water and they pumped and bailed but it was coming in faster than they could handle it, so, finally the skipper said to his helper, who wasn't wrapped very tight, as they say, 'This boat is sinking, if you know any prayers, you better say 'em.' The helper allowed that he didn't know any prayers, as such, but he said that he used to live next door to a Catholic church and he could hear what they were saying, sometimes. The skipper said 'That's more than I can offer — go to it.' With that, the helper got down on his knees in the bottom of the boat and said, 'Under B-15 . . .'"

The milking was done by this time, and we were walk-

ing back to the house. "Back a few years ago, Reverend, I got lost up in Macwahoc. No road map, couldn't see any signs, so I stopped and asked this feller who didn't have a full sea-bag, either, and he had no idea how to direct me to Bangor, so I started to drive away. Hadn't any more than got under way when I heard him hollering and, looking in the mirror, I saw him and another feller running after my car. 'Course I stopped, and he came up alongside my car and said 'This is my cousin, he don't know the way, either.'

"After awhile, I came to a gas station and got directions. The feller that ran the gas station told me about a tourist who got turned around in the same area, said this feller and his wife were driving around and all of a sudden he was faced with three roads and no signs. After awhile, he decided to stop at a little store and ask directions. Well, that store-keeper was a typical old Downeaster, mighty short on words and all. The feller left his wife in the car, went into the store and asked, 'There is a road out here that goes off to the right, can you tell me where it goes?'

"The old storekeeper simply said: 'Macwahoc.' 'Course this didn't mean anything to the tourist so he said: 'That road that goes straight, where does that go?' The store-keeper answered: 'Passadumkeag.' Still confused, the tourist said: 'Okay. If I take the left fork, where will it take me?' The old feller simply answered, 'Wytopitlock.' The tourist got back in his car, his wife asked if he found out where they were, and he replied, 'Good Lord, no, that feller can't speak a word of English!' "

The Reverend commented, "It's hard to imagine even a tourist who never saw a place with an Indian name before. Look, I've got to get going, that lawn of mine is growing all the while I'm standing here."

As he started down the driveway with my lawnmower in tow, I called after him, "You know, if you wait a month or so, the first frost will kill the grass and you can just go along and kick it over."

He just looked over his shoulder and waved, but I knew he was thinking about giving me a sermon on sloth.

They call Maine the four season state, but as far as I can see, there are only two seasons: winter and the Fourth of July.

Fall is probably my favorite time of the year. The weather is usually quite pleasant, being warm during the day and plenty cool enough to sleep at night. Matter of fact, 'bout the only fault I can find with Fall is that Winter is next on the schedule, and not far away at that. Each day is a little shorter than the day before 'til finally it's Winter and we don't hardly get a day at all. Winter days in Maine seem more like nights that just ain't quite as dark.

The deer hunting season opened two days ago, so a bunch of us got together and drove up to my camp on Mopang Stream. We saw one deer on the way into the camp and Jake Morgan made a half-hearted attempt to get out of the car and take a shot at it, but it was moving so fast I doubt that a bullet from that old .30-.30 of his could have caught it, anyway. Besides, no one wants to shoot a deer the first day of hunting season. If the weather is too warm it's apt to spoil before you can get it back home, and, if you leave it hanging outside the camp, a bear might get it some dark night.

These hunting trips are 'bout all the same, more deer are killed in the camp than in the woods. When a bunch of hunters get going on game stories, the hair and blood gets pretty deep on the camp floor. I know for a fact that Rufe Collins hasn't killed a deer for at least 10 years, but by the tales he tells you would think he was Maine's answer to Buffalo Bill.

As usual, after supper we were all sitting around the table playing penny-ante poker and trying to top each other. Poor old Diogenes wouldn't have hung around there very long.

There is one in the crowd who doesn't join in on the games or the story telling, or anything else for that matter. I've known Uriah Boardman for years and I've never known him to do anything but sit around and concentrate on doing nothing. He reminds me of that old duffer they tell about who went to a summer resort and just sat around, doing nothing all the while he was there. That particular year, they had a brand new Social Director and she was some busy making sure everyone was having a good time doing something. Well, as I say, this old duffer was there mostly because his son had talked him into going there with him, thinking it would do him good. By and by, that young Social Director spied the old feller just sitting on a bench all alone doing nothing, so she rushed right over and started talking to him.

"Would you like to play tennis?" she asked.

The old feller simply said, "Nope — tried it once, didn't like it."

Not being one to give up too easy, she asked, "How about some badminton?"

The old feller said again, "Nope, tried it once, didn't like it."

Then the young lady said, "Okay, then, why don't you come with me, and we'll go swimming?"

The old feller said, "No, tried that once, too, didn't like that either, but that's my son over there, he might like to go swimming with you."

The young lady was a little put out with him by now, and replied, "He's an only child, I'll bet."

Stan Pinkham was dealing the cards, and telling about

the first time he ever drove over Route #9, what we call "The Airline." It runs between Bangor and Calais through one of the most desolate areas of Maine. Years ago it was narrow and crooked, wasn't even tarred for long stretches at a time.

"Never saw anything like it," Stan was saying. "Miles and miles of nothing but miles and miles. If a man ever got broke down on that road in a new car, by the time anyone else came along they would probably tow his car directly to a museum. There was one real bad piece of road, I saw the sign that said: ROAD UNDER REPAIR. What it didn't say was that they had taken it into the shop!

"At the time, I had a 1937 Chevrolet, which I thought would go most anywhere, but she went into a water hole clear up to her running boards and fetched up solid. Yes, Grover, a flush beats a straight.

"Well, there I was, figuring out my next move, when a feller came along with a team of horses and wanted to know if I could use some help. I told him that I'd like to trade even, the car for one of his horses, but he couldn't see that, said he'd twitch me out of there for five dollars. I thought his price was a little steep, but paid him anyway. He hooked that team on and they just walked off with that car like it was an empty buggy. 'Course, I thought I'd been taken and I was not too happy about it, so just before I drove away I said to him, 'You know, for five dollars a tow you could hang around here and make a fortune hauling cars out of there day and night.'

" 'I do a lot of towing during the day, but not at night,' he said. 'At night I haul the water for that hole!' "

"How come none of you guys have seen any deer yet?" asked Uriah.

Grover answered, "All I've seen so far is a couple of tracks, but 'course that only shows where they were, and I want to know where they are now."

Ira added, "I still think the deer are scarce on account of the moose, deer just won't stay around where there are moose."

That argument has been going on for years, so to keep it from starting up again I said, "I don't know why it is, but it seems to me that there are less deer now than when I built this camp. That first year I had the best luck I ever had before or since. I was standing out by the woodpile when I saw this doe, walking along at the edge of the clearing, and it was the strangest thing I ever saw. There was a big buck right behind her, holding her tail in his mouth! Real quick I ran into the camp, grabbed my rifle, stuffed one shell into it, ran out and drew a bead on that buck's head and fired. For some reason I pulled her off to the right and that bullet cut that doe's tail clean off. She took off into the woods but the buck just stood there, so I walked up to him and it was just what I figured — he was stone blind! Well, I didn't have another bullet, so I just grabbed that tail, led him right up to the camp door and hit him in the head with a pole axe."

Ira gave me that look which said without words, okay, you asked for it, and he began: "The best luck I ever had was the time I went into the woods with only one bullet to my name. That was during the Great Depression and everything was hard to come by, even ammunition.

"As I say," he continued, "I was walking along, wondering how I was going to get through the winter with very little money and not much food in the larder. Suddenly, right in front of me, not 20 yards away, were two beautiful silver foxes. Even in those days a silver fox pelt was worth a pretty penny, and here I was with two of them within range, but only one bullet. Standing between them was a big flat rock, shaped like an old-fashioned gravestone. 'Course, I was some tempted to play it safe and shoot one of them foxes, but, instead, I aimed right at that rock and fired. The bullet hit the rock, broke in two and killed both foxes. The kick from the gun knocked me backwards into a brook, and when I regained my senses, my right hand was on a beaver's tail, my left hand was on a mink's head, and my pants pockets were so full of trout that a button popped off my fly and killed a partridge!"